HANDEL'S MESSIAH

for the Beginning Pianist

WITH DOWNLOADABLE MP3s

DAVID DUTKANICZ

DOVER PUBLICATIONS, INC.

Mineola, New York

All music available as downloadable MP3s!

Go to www.doverpublications.com/0486839109
to access these files.

Bibliographical Note

Handel's Messiah for the Beginning Pianist with Downloadable MP3s
is a new work, first published by Dover Publications, Inc. in 2019.

International Standard Book Number

ISBN-13: 978-0-486-83910-3
ISBN-10: 0-486-83910-9

Manufactured in the United States by LSC Communications
83910901
www.doverpublications.com

2 4 6 8 10 9 7 5 3 1

2019

Contents

Introduction

Whether I was in my body or out of my body
as I wrote it I know not. God knows.
—Handel on composing the "Hallelujah!" chorus

George Frideric Handel (1685–1759) found great inspiration and composed all fifty-three movements of *Messiah* in only twenty-four days. Audiences have cherished the work since its 1742 premiere, making it one of the most frequently performed works ever written. The "Hallelujah!" chorus is universally recognized, and other movements such as "For unto Us a Child Is Born" and "Glory to God" frame the holidays alongside the most famous of Christmas carols.

The aim of *Handel's Messiah for the Beginning Pianist* is to make this wonderful music accessible to a wider audience. Movements have been carefully selected and arranged for the beginning pianist. Fingerings are suggested and should be customized for each individual. Every piece draws upon the wealth of Handel's original score and serves as a tool in developing technique as well as musicality.

HANDEL'S MESSIAH
for the Beginning Pianist

MOVEMENT NO. 1
Overture

Messiah is a collection of fifty-three movements known collectively as an "oratorio." It is presented onstage without costumes or scenery, as opposed to operas and plays. The Overture serves as an introduction to the work. Play slowly, and be mindful of the sharps in measures 5 and 6 (A# and C#).

Slowly

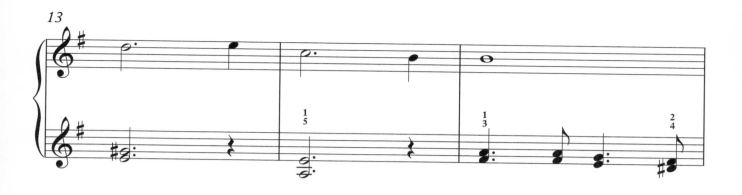

MOVEMENT NO. 2
Comfort Ye My People

This movement is a "recitative." It is sung by a solo voice and is similar to a narrator providing details and unfolding an account of the events. Note the tempo: *larghetto* (slightly faster than *largo*). Play slowly, but with enough movement and expression to keep the music from dragging.

MOVEMENT NO. 3
Every Valley Shall Be Exalted

Handel uses a musical device known as "imitation" to express the text of this movement. The melody in measures 1 and 2 (sung by a tenor) is repeated in measures 4 and 5 (an octave higher by the orchestra). This creates an echo, evoking the hills and valleys that are being praised.

MOVEMENT NO. 4

And the Glory of the Lord

When playing this movement, be mindful of the changes in dynamics and the number of voices. With one (solo) voice, the work opens at *mf*. When the chorus enters (measures 4 through 7), voices are added and the dynamic level is raised to *f*. It returns to the original *mf* in measure 7, with two voices this time.

Allegro moderato

MOVEMENT NO. 5

Thus Saith the Lord

This recitative for bass soloist contains the text "Thus saith the Lord . . . I will shake the heavens and the earth, the sea and the dry land." This dramatic lyric is given a fitting melody and is played here by the left hand. Envision a deep bass voice singing these notes, with the right hand providing the accompaniment originally performed by an orchestra.

Andante

8

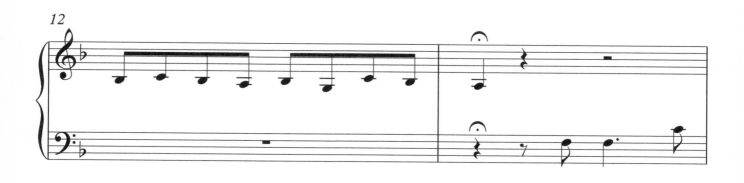

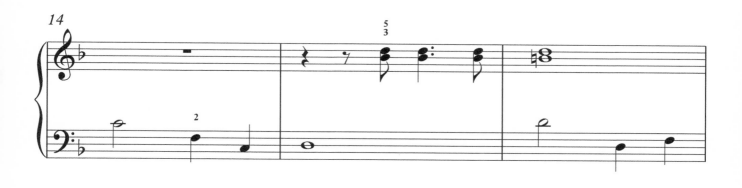

MOVEMENT NO. 6

But Who May Abide
the Day of His Coming?

The austere tone of the previous work continues here in this "air." Much like an aria in opera, it is a short movement designed to highlight the melodic and expressive talents of a singer. An air also interprets the text to a higher degree than a recitative, which states its text in a more spoken tone.

Andante larghetto

MOVEMENT NO. 11
The People That Walked in Darkness

Before practicing this movement, look over the accidentals that appear throughout (e.g., G# in measure 1; D#, C#, and D natural in measure 2). Note that they each push the melody forward by going up a half-step to the next note. Also, be mindful of the page turn at the bottom. There is no need to rush, and you can resume playing when you are ready.

Unhurried

(Turn page.)

11

For unto Us a Child Is Born

In addition to the famous "Hallelujah!" this lovely movement is another holiday favorite. The entire chorus joins in singing "For unto us a Child is born, unto us a Son is given." Note the repetition and gradual rise of the melody in the right hand from measures 2 through 6. This is a musical sequence, where short melodic material is repeated in a rising or falling motion.

Andante allegro

MOVEMENT NO. 13
Pastoral Symphony

This movement is known as a "symphony" because it is an instrumental solo and refers to the orchestra performing it. It is also named "pastoral" because it is long drones (notes held in the left hand), which imitate the pipes of the countryside. Play in a peaceful manner and at a calm yet moving pace.

Moderato

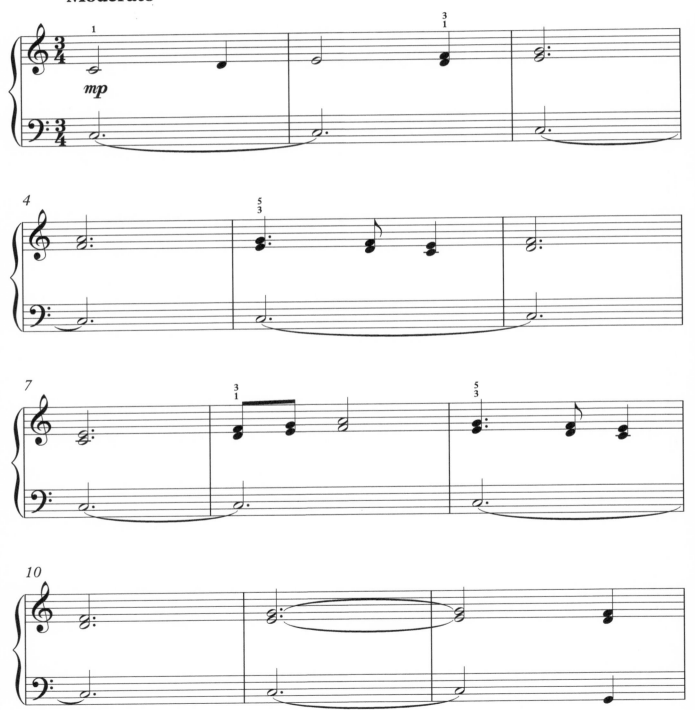

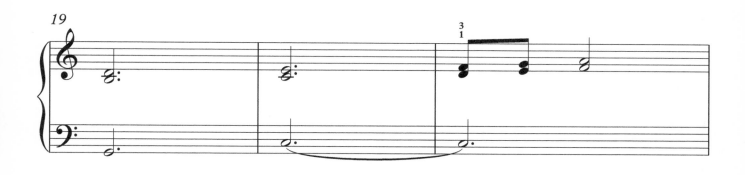

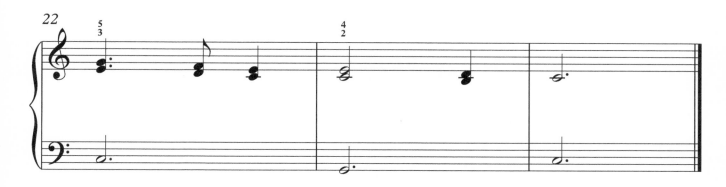

MOVEMENT NO. 15
And the Angel Said unto Them

This recitative is for a soprano soloist and orchestra. It is a perfect example of how speech is used to create the music, both melodically by the inflection of the voice and rhythmically by the words themselves. Play at a spoken tempo, mimicking speech with clarity in your tone production.

At a spoken tempo

MOVEMENT NO. 16

And Suddenly There Was with the Angel

With very little pause, this recitative is performed immediately after the previous and is also for a soprano soloist. The first three measures are a short introduction played by the orchestra, and the voice enters on the eighth note of measure 3. As with other recitatives, play the notes clearly and distinctly as if they were being narrated.

Unhurried

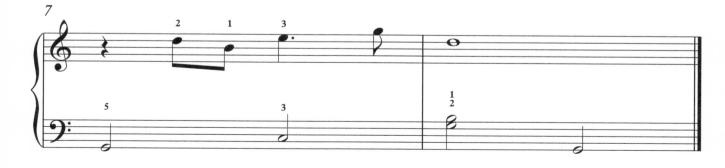

Glory to God

Handel composes a majestic movement here, with the choir angelically singing a familiar text: "Glory to God in the highest, and peace on Earth, good will toward men." Play in a regal manner, with an upbeat and celebratory tempo.

Allegro

MOVEMENT NO. 18
Rejoice Greatly, O Daughter of Zion

This air for soprano provided a chance to display vocal master. In the right-hand melody, pay attention to measures 5 and 6 and imagine a smooth singing of the phrase. Soloists train to perform each note evenly and smoothly, as should you.

Allegro moderato

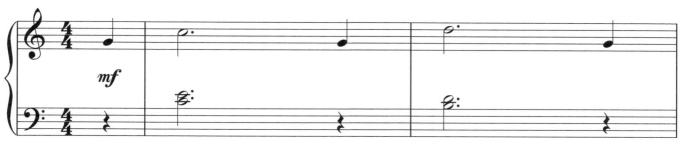

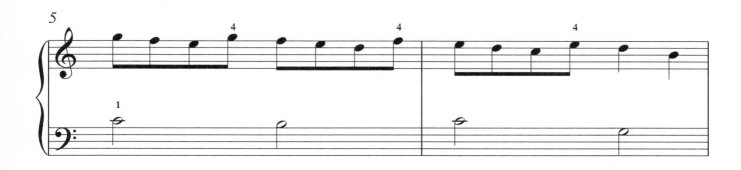

He Shall Feed His Flock like a Shepherd

There are four voices in a chorus. In descending order of range, they are soprano, alto, tenor, and bass. Each voice possesses a color palette unique to its range, and Handel assigned different solos based on his interpretation. This air is for an alto soloist, which has a lower range of notes than the other female voice, soprano.

Slowly

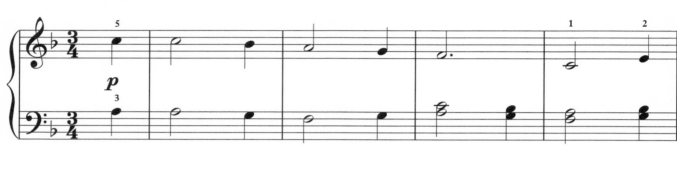

Behold the Lamb of God

Just as in movement 3, Handel uses imitation as a compositional device. The right-hand melody of measure 1 is repeated here in the left-hand of measure 2. Both should sound even and identical in tempo.

He Was Despised

Messiah is divided into three sections, with the second containing movements 22–44. It also is referred to as "The Passion." Play with a somber character, using the held rests (measures 2 and 6) to add to the feeling of the work.

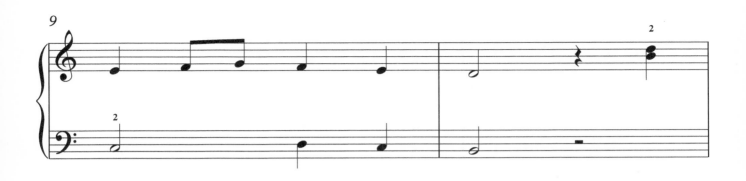

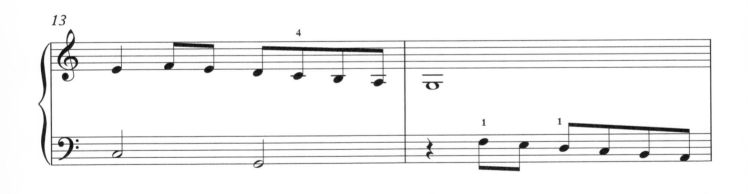

Surely He Hath Borne Our Griefs

The tempo marking *Largo e staccato* means "slowly and detached." In musical performance, the detachment should be a brief space or breath between the notes. Add the pedal to help sustain the tones, but remove the pedal between the notes.

Largo e staccato

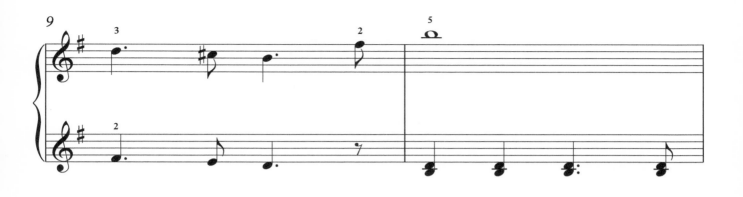

MOVEMENT NO. 25

And with His Stripes We Are Healed

In a fugue, a short theme known as a "subject" is repeated by a number of voices. In this example, the first voice the short melody on an E, and the second repeats it but begins on an E. (In the original, all four voices enter in and take turns singing the melody.) Also, review the accidentals before practicing and listen to how they heighten the emotion of the work.

Moderato

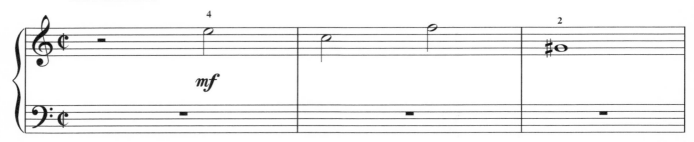

All We, like Sheep, Have Gone Astray

The position and control of your wrists are very important to how your notes sound. In passages that require the hand to reposition (such as the right hand of measures 4–5), the wrist must be properly placed to allow the fingers to comfortably strike the keys. When practicing, plan the motion of the wrist in addition to what fingers are being used.

Moderato

All They That See Him, Laugh Him to Scorn

This movement is filled with accidentals, which Handel uses to switch between minor chords and their relative majors. The F-naturals outline a D-minor chord (D-F-A), while the return of the F-sharps ends the piece on a D-major chord (D-F#-A). This change of a tonal center is known as "modulation."

But Thou Didst Not Leave His Soul

The text of *Messiah* was compiled by Charles Jennens, who was a landowner and patron of the arts. He wrote the libretto to several of Handel's oratorios (and edited many critical editions of Shakespeare's plays). All the texts are taken from the King James Bible, with many (such as this) taken from the Book of Psalms.

Andante larghetto

Lift Up Your Heads, O Ye Gates

This majestic chorus is in reference to the Ascension, with the verse reading "Lift up your heads, O ye gates; and be ye lift up, ye everlasting doors; and the King of glory shall come in." Note how the dotted rhythms, especially in measure 3, create a sense of procession compared to straight rhythms.

Moderato

Thou Art Gone Up on High

Bass solos are full of deep and resonant notes that shine in their lower registers. The left hand here is playing the vocal line of the bass solo. Practice playing lyrically, with the notes smoothly flowing one to another as a voice. This can be achieved by beginning at a slow tempo and then progressing as your fingers feel confident with the notes.

Allegro moderato

How Beautiful Are the Feet of Them

The text of this movement opens "How beautiful are the feet of them that preach the gospel of peace," referencing the long journeys of the disciples. Play with a light tone and at a slow tempo.

Slowly

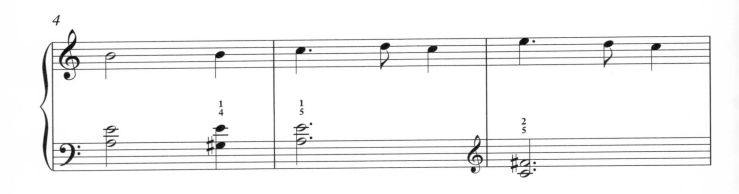

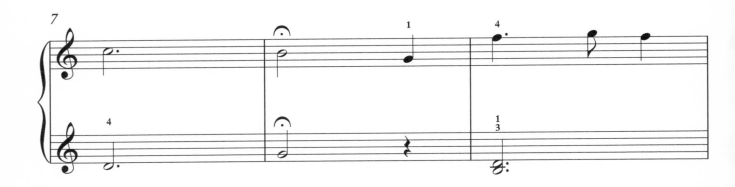

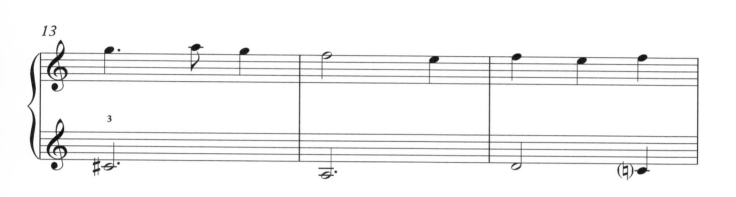

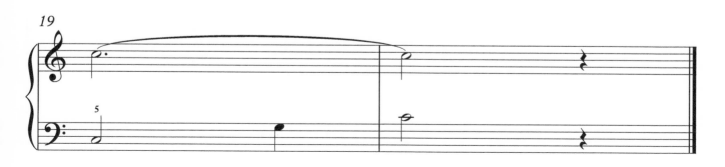

MOVEMENT NO. 44
Hallelujah!

This is the most famous movement of *Messiah*, and it has been bringing audiences to their feet since its London premiere. According to tradition (and legend), King George II was so moved by the opening notes of the chorus that he rose to his feet. To this day, it is customary for audiences to stand during the performance of this movement.

I Know That My Redeemer Liveth

Part of Handel's artistry was creating a dialogue between the soloists and the orchestra. An example can be found in measures 11–14, with the soprano soloist (played by the right hand) being answered and echoed by the orchestra (played by the left hand).

Larghetto

Since by Man Came Death

This movement opens as a chorale, with three- and four-voice textures singing in unison rhythms. Review the accidentals before playing, especially in measure 5. And remember that when playing more than one note per hand, to play both as one voice (striking the notes at the same time).

Grave

The Trumpet Shall Sound

The grand fanfare of the melody paints the imagery of the verse "The trumpet shall sound, and the dead shall arise." Also, note the tempo marking: *pomposo* means "in a stately and dignified manner" (not "pompous").

MOVEMENT NO. 52

If God Be for Us,
Who Can Be against Us?

In this air for soprano, Handel offers a last personal reflection before the finale of the work. The simple yet powerful nature of the music contrasts the previous movements, while preparing for the grandness of the closing music.

Larghetto

Worthy Is the Lamb That Was Slain

(OPENING)

The final movement of *Messiah* opens with a slow and somber chorale, which does grow into a much grander finale. Even one of Handel's toughest critics was impressed by this movement and said, "Had Handel never composed another chorus . . . he might with justice have been ranked at the head of musical composers."

Largo

Amen

Handel closes his glorious oratorio with an extended setting of the word *Amen*. The theme begins simply and is developed for over eighty measures before ending on a grand cadence. In this arrangement, the first two entrances of the theme are presented and should be played in imitation of each other (i.e., equal in tempo, tone, dynamics, and expression).

Allegro moderato